Macramé Hanging Plant

20 Ideas for Beginners with HD Illustrations to Create Wall Hanging Models to Decorate Your Home & Garden

(Basic Knots and Tutorials Included)

Catherine Ludemberg

Table of Content

Introduction 1

Section 1: A Basic Introduction to Macramé For Beginners 3

    The Origin of Macramé 4

    Getting Started In Using Macramé For Your Designs 5

How To Start a Macramé Wall Hanging 11

    Basic Knots To Master... 11

    Half and Double Half Hitch Knots 16

    How To Hang a Large Macramé Wall Design 18

Section 2: 20 DIY Macramé Wall Hanging Projects(With HD Illustrations to Create Wall Hanging Models to Decorate Your Home & Garden) 20

    1: DIY Macramé Wall Hanging (#1) 21

    2: DIY Macramé Wall Hanging (#2) 26

    3: DIY Macramé Wall Hanging (#3) 30

    4: DIY Macramé Wall Hanging (#4) 33

    5: DIY Mini Macramé Wall Hanging (#5).............. 39

    6: Home Woven Wall Hanging in 5 Minutes 42

    7: Macramé Fiber Wall Art 45

8: Macramé Wall Hanging in 20 Minutes 47

9: DIY Macramé Wall Hanging (#6) 51

10: Macramé Christmas Wreath 54

11: DIY Ring Wall Hanging 57

12: DIY Yarn Wall Hanging 60

13: Yarn Leftovers Wall Hanging 63

14: Copper Wool Roving Macramé Wall Hanging . 65

15: Yarn Wall Hanging 70

16: DIY Yarn Wall Hanging in 30 Minutes 76

17: DIY Macramé Plant Hanger 79

18: DIY Macramé Wall Hanging (#7) 84

19: DIY Modern Yarn Hanging 88

20: DIY Modern Macramé Wall Hanging 94

Conclusion 97

Introduction

Do you want to learn how to create beautiful macramé wall hangings that stand out?

Or perhaps even though you want to learn, you are curious about how difficult it is to create macramé knots?

And are you looking for a book that will teach you everything you need to know about macramé?

Well, if this is you:

<u>You Are About To Discover How To Design Macramé Wall Hanging Patterns Through Basic Knots Along With Illustrations On How To Create Wall Hanging Models To Decorate Your Home & Garden</u>

This book is here to take all the mystery out of the macramé process. Anyone can do this! Yes, I know you've got doubts, but that's why this book is here.

<u>By the time you complete reading this book, you'll have:</u>

- Basic knowledge of what macramé is all about
- Learned how to make simple knots within the shortest time possible!

- The know-how to choose the best ropes and other supplies for completely unique designs
- Be able to design beautiful and affordable DIY macramé wall hangings for your decor or commercial purposes

Even if you've never considered yourself a craftsman or woman, this book will turn you into a great macramé designer without trying too hard!

Let's get started:

Section 1
A Basic Introduction to Macramé For Beginners

Macramé is a technique of creating knots to create beautiful decorative pieces. These knots are mostly hand-crafted, and the craft usually involves very few tools, just the cord and mounting ring with which to secure the design in place.

From where did this knot-making craft technique originate?

The Origin of Macramé

The prevailing consensus is that macramé styling originated from the Arabic word 'migramah,' which loosely translates to 'fringe.' In the 13th century, Arab weavers used macramé knots to make decorative fringes, particularly on veils and shawls.

That said:

Many people also believe that the Chinese invented the decorative knot-tying technique to make their ceremonial garments, lanterns, and wall hangings. Chinese textiles from back then usually had several knots—for instance, the pan.

During the 13th century, Arabic designs spread to Europe, which ultimately became a preferable crafting technique for sailors. The sailors used Macramé aboard their ships for decoration and barter trade involving knotted products such as hats, belts, and hammocks.

The knot-tying design became a popular hobby for adorning textiles throughout the Victorian era, but it only achieved global recognition in the 70s.'

Let us now learn how to get started:

Getting Started In Using Macramé For Your Designs

Let us start with what you will need to get started:

Required Tools and Materials For Macramé Designs

Here are some of the most commonly used tools and materials for wall hanging macramé:

- Macramé cord or rope
- Metal or wood dowel
- Tape measure
- Scissors painters tape
- Masking tape or painters tape

Let's discuss a few of these materials and supplies in detail:

Dowels

You need this for attaching your macramé cords. You can have a dowel made from driftwood, a wooden branch, or just a plain stick you bought from the DIY store—or made yourself.

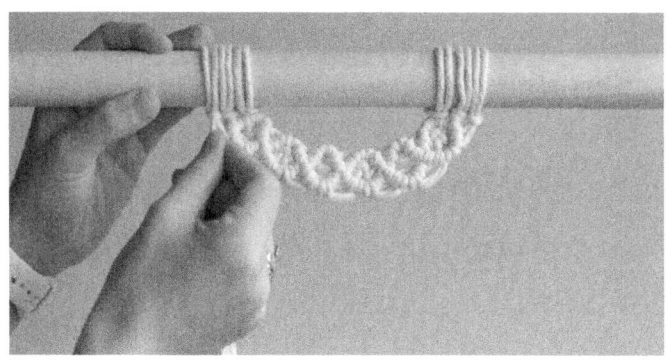

Ropes or Cords

The most recommended cord is the **three-strand rope** that perfectly holds most knot shapes. The three-strand rope is also stiffer and quite tough, thus ensuring that designs can hold their shape well.

You can also consider the **single-strand cord** but only when incorporating a lot of fringe in your macramé hanging. However, the single strand cord doesn't hold knot shapes that well —at least not compared to the 3-ply— but it produces a class of unique designs based on the look you want to achieve with your design.

If you love colored knotting cords, try eco-friendly **Bobbiny recycled Macramé cords** that yield stunning and unique designs. If you need larger macramé hangings, try the 3-Ply ropes instead. Ensure you tape the end of the 3-Ply cords to keep them from unraveling.

Macramé Board

A macramé board is a secure place where you set your project for knotting. You can make a macramé board from various materials such as corkboard, two pieces of cardboard joined together, or a piece of polyurethane. The rule of the thumb is to get a secure surface that allows you to insert pins into it effortlessly.

Try making the macramé board around 1-feet, 12 inches square, and thick enough to accommodate insertion of a corsage pin or T pin without the pin sticking out the other side.

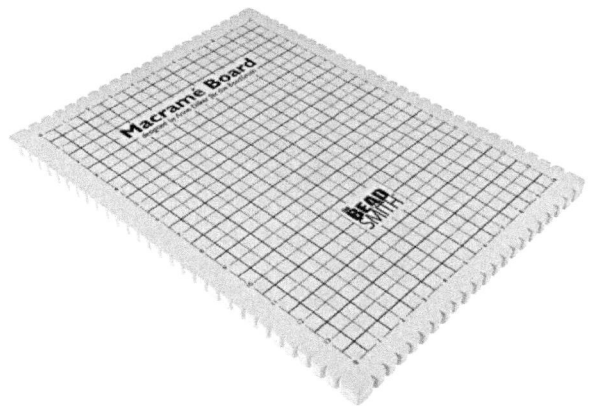

Besides choosing your ropes and dowels, you'll also need to know the special terms used in macramé making, such as:

Knotting cords and Knot-bearing cords:

These two cord types refer to the set of ropes or cords you will use when making whichever stitch you want.

The knot-bearing cords are a set of cords where you wrap the knotting cords around. The knot-bearing and knotting cord might change in different steps of your project, but the pattern will reflect this.

Sennit:

This is a set of a particular stitch worked in repeat. For instance, if you're to work 6 half knot stitches back to back in a row, you'll be said to create a sennit of 6 half knots.

How To Start a Macramé Wall Hanging

The initial step is to decide what to use for your macramé hanging, whether it's a piece of driftwood, a pipe, or a dowel.

If using dowels, try buying those of different lengths and diameters from whichever type of wood and color you want. For round wall macramé hangings, select a metal ring from the different available sizes of metal bases.

After choosing your preferred base, you will proceed to attach your macramé cords using commonly used knotting cords.

Now that we're talking about knots, macramé stitching has some commonly used knots you should know:

Basic Knots To Master

The most commonly used macramé knots are:

Lark's head knot

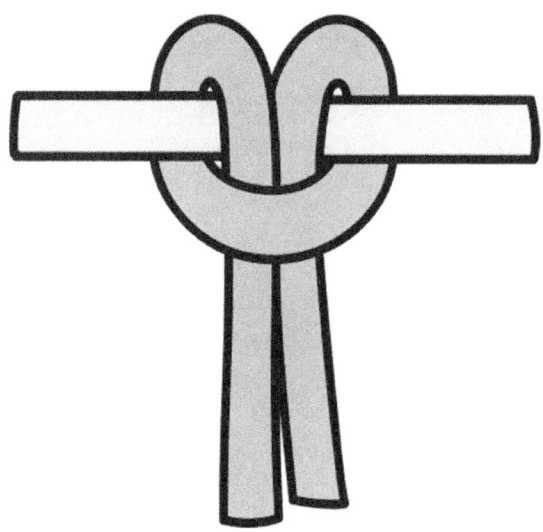

The most common use of this knot is to attach your knotting cord to a ring or dowel. Here are the steps to follow when making the Lark's Head Knot:

1. Begin by folding your knotting cord in half to make a loop.

2. Then put the folded macramé cord on a working surface. Ensure your loop points downwards while the ends of the macramé cord point up.

3. Now put your ring or dowel on top of the folded macramé cord above your loop.

4. Start pulling the loop over the ring or dowel and then pull the macramé cord ends through the loop.

5. Finally, pull down to make the knot tighter.

Reverse Lark's head knot

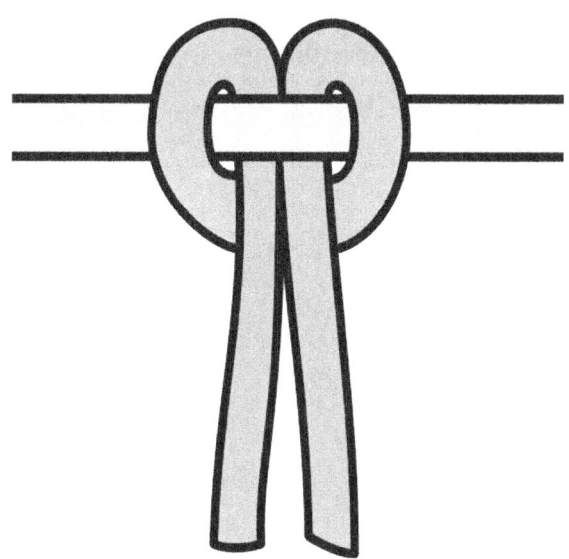

Also called the Cow Hitch Knot, the Reverse Lark's Head knot is the same as making the Lark's Head knot but on reverse. Here's how to go about it:

1. Start by folding the knotting cord in half, then put the folded macramé cord on a working surface.

2. Position the ends of the macramé cord pointing down and the loop pointing up.

3. Then put your ring or dowel on top of the folded macramé cord just slightly above your loop.

4. Now start pulling the loop down over your ring or dowel

5. Next, pull the ends of the macramé cord up and down through the loop and tighten it by pulling down.

Half Knot

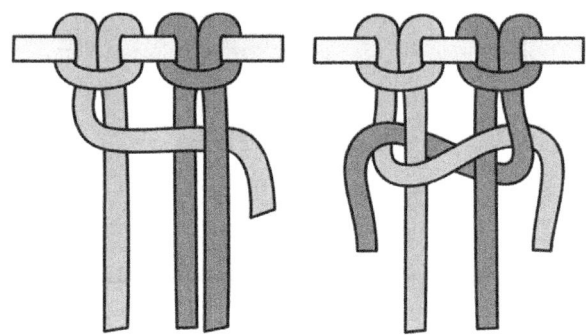

These knots are used to make **sinnet**, described as a column of two or even more half-square or square knots. A sennit of half knots produces a natural spiral required in plant hanger DIY projects, as shown in the diagram below:

To make this knot, you'll need to work with four macramé cords: the first two outer cords being the knotting cords, whereas the other two will be the knot-bearing macramé cords.

Here's how to make the knot:

1. Begin by bringing the knotting cord on the left side over the two other cords and now beneath the knotting cord on the right.

2. Then bring the knotting cord on the right to the left side just beneath the two other cords and over the knotting code on the left.

3. To secure the knot, just pull the knotting cords quite firmly.

Square Knot

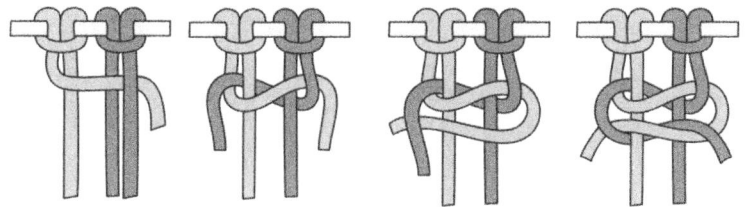

This knot is described as the completion of the Half Knot in that the initial steps resemble those of the Half Knot. However, you have to work a second Half Knot with the opposite knotting cords to finish the knot.

Here's how to go about it:

1. Do steps 1 and 2 in the previous Half Knot.
2. Continue by bringing the knotting cord from the right side to the left one over the knot-bearing cords, and below the knotting cord on the left.
3. Now bring the knotting cord from the left to the right, just beneath the knot-bearing cords and over the knotting cord on the right.

To secure the knot, pull the knot-bearing cords together.

Half and Double Half Hitch Knots

You can work these knots in various designs, whether diagonally, vertically, or horizontally, and with various knot-bearing and knotting cords.

You can also work them from right to left or left to right, making them the most versatile knot in macramé making. A double half is just two progressive half hitch knots. In other words, you work the knotting steps twice, one after the other.

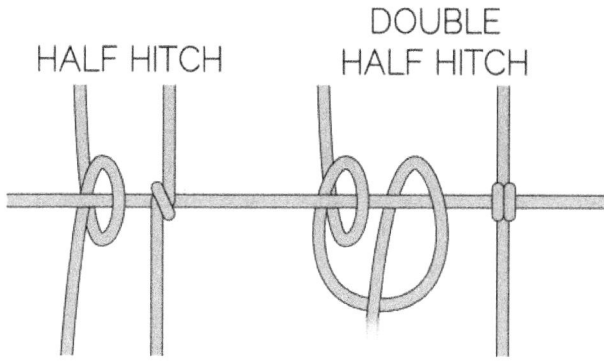

Here are steps to follow when tying a Double Half Hitch Knot at a diagonal and around a hoop.

1. Put the cord hanging at the backside of your hoop.
2. Grab the end of the cording and then start pulling it towards you.
3. Loop the cord over the hoop and then pull it to the left side
4. Repeat the last two steps, but now pull the end of your cord up through your hoop.
5. Now tighten the knot.

Tying Two Half Hitches

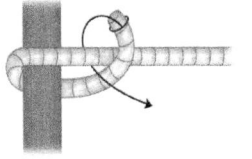 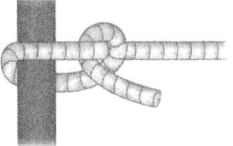

① Wrap the rope around a support   ② Pass the end through the loop

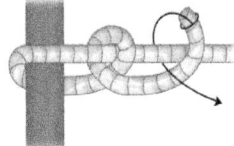 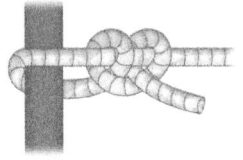

③ Wrap it around the standing part   ④ Tighten to complete

Once done knotting your macramé wall hanging, it's time to hang them on your wall. There are a few ideas for that!

How To Hang a Large Macramé Wall Design

When you want to hang a large macramé wall design, try using a hanging rope on both ends of your driftwood dowel through a suitable knot, and then use a nail to support the design on the wall.

You can also use 2-3 long nails on your wall while sticking out a few inches, then rest your macramé wall hanging across the nails until almost fully hidden. However, you might need to use a level to ensure that the nails are quite nice and straight. Be aware that some types of walls may also demand the use of screws and drywall anchors instead.

If hanging your design in the workplace, consider buying a rolling clothing rack or using a ring hung or dowel. Try hanging the macramé design from a secure piece of wall or furniture.

In addition, you can also get a suction cup or use an over-the-door wreath hanger.

With that basic knowledge, let's add some Boho Spirit with these 20 ideas on creating wall hanging models to decorate your home & garden:

Section 2

20 DIY Macramé Wall Hanging Projects

(With HD Illustrations to Create Wall Hanging Models to Decorate Your Home & Garden)

1: DIY Macramé Wall Hanging (#1)

Tools and supplies

Glue gun

Scissors

Cardboard

12-inch Long brass pipe

6mm cord, yarn color choice

Instructions

1. Begin by cutting your cardboard to the required length of macramé wall hanging.

2. Then loosely wrap your yarn color choice around the cardboard six times. Once done, cut all the loops simultaneously at the end of your cardboard.

3. Repeat the above step with extra colors, or instead, double or triple the total number of times you wrap around your cardboard if using only one or two colors. You should have a total of 18 pieces of differently colored yarn.

4. Now fold one piece of yarn or cord in half to make a loop. Now wrap the yarn around your brass pipe and pull the two ends of the cord through the loop. Ensure to make a tight knot.

5. Repeat the step with the rest of the yarn cords as you alternate the colors to create a unique design.

6. After tying all the yarn pieces around the pipe, cut another piece of yarn to hang the brass pipe, depending on how long you want the pipe to hang.

7. At this point, tie one end of the knotting cord yarn around individual ends of the pipe and secure the yarn with hot glue. Check if you have all the pieces of the frayed edges of the yarn properly glued down.

8. Now you can hang your well-crafted macramé wall hanging!

2: DIY Macramé Wall Hanging (#2)

Tools and supplies

Large wooden beads

Acrylic paint

Painters tape

Scissors

Paintbrush

Wooden dowel

70 yards of rope (approx 63m)

Instructions

1. Begin by attaching a dowel to your wall, with easy-to-remove command hooks.

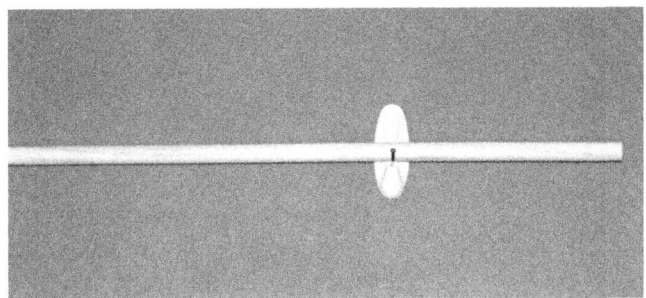

2. Then cut the knotting cord or rope to approx 12-foot pieces. Tie the rope through the lark head knots, and tie again through the half hitch knot across the design.

3. At this point, tie double half hitch knots in a diagonal direction along all your rope pieces. Attach some wooden beads at

various strategic locations and then tie the knot fully.

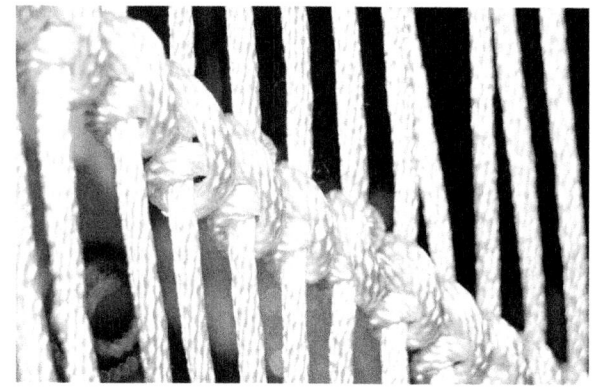

4. Now tie some switch knots with about 4 ropes pieces each.

5. Complete the design with double hitch knots and finally bring those knots along diagonally.

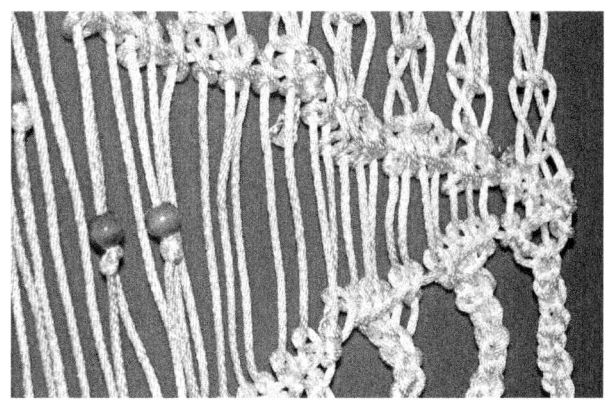

6. Use the scissors to trim any unnecessary ends of rope pieces. Ensure you've fully tightened the roped before hanging the macramé design.

3: DIY Macramé Wall Hanging (#3)

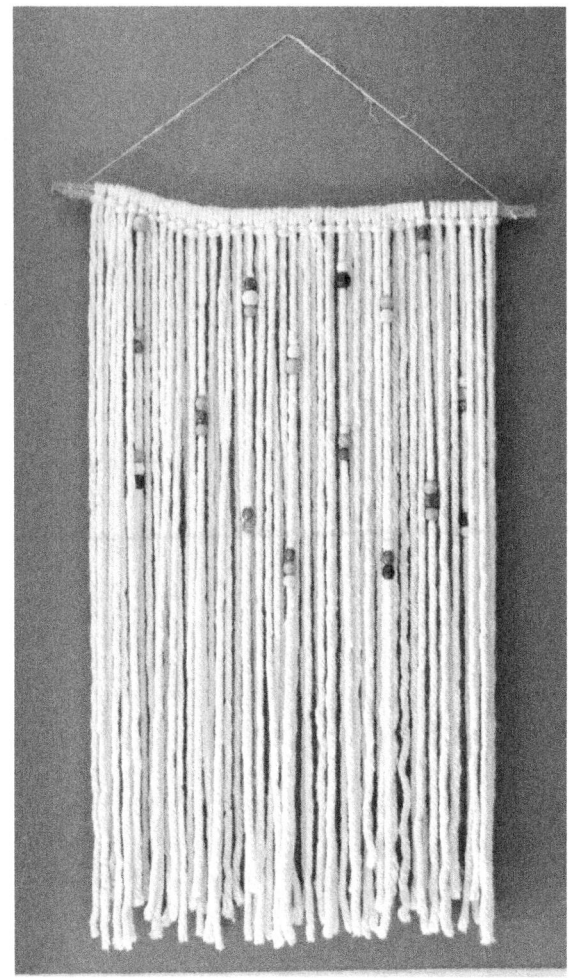

Tools and supplies

Tape

Measuring stick

Wood beads

Drill

Jute

27" wide driftwood or stick

2 rolls of yarn

Instructions

1. Start by drilling 2 holes in your wood rod — for hanging at any end.

2. Then cut your yard cord based on the size of your rod.

3. Now loop the yarn all over the wood rod, then pull the yarn through to get around 1.5 inches of wood display on each side. You might have to drill larger holes.

4. To make the hanger, obtain your jute and tie knots at each end.

5. At this point, trim down your pieces of yarn. You just need to trim the yarn a few pieces at a time to make an uneven bottom. The macramé wall hanging should be about 33 inches.

4: DIY Macramé Wall Hanging (#4)

Tools and supplies

Scissors

Dark Walnut stain

Dowel

Cut end cotton mop refill

Maximizer cotton mop refill

Instructions

1. Begin by cutting your dowel to 15 inches lower wooden piece and 15 inches for the top wooden piece.

2. Stain them using the dark walnut wood stain, then open the cotton mop refill and cut its ends off. Cut a little chunk of this for your project.

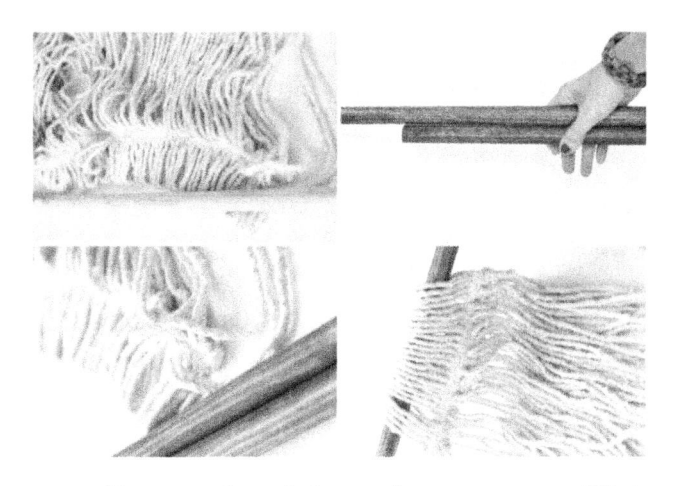

3. Slip your dowel through your mop refill, just on the top hooks. Get duck tape and secure your dowel to a flat surface to keep it from moving as you work.

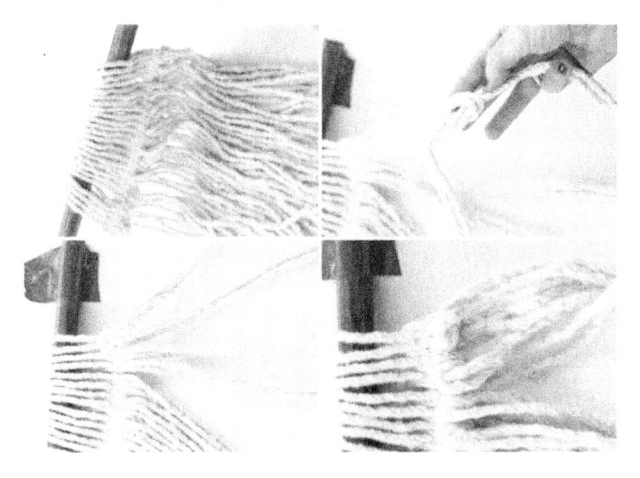

4. Now separate the yarn pieces into fours and then make a knot with two yarn pieces. Begin making the knots.

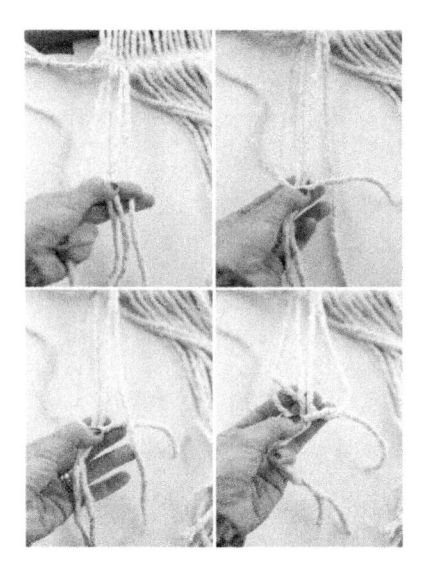

5. Make tying knots for the first row and the same knots for the second and third knots.

6. Open the next bag of the mop refill. Then pull out two yarn pieces from the bunch and create a hanger for your wall hanging.

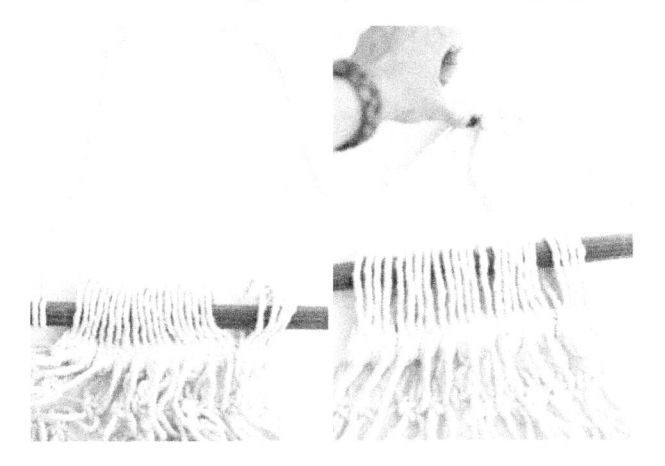

7. Finally, pull the whole piece of mop refill through the center of your macramé wall design.

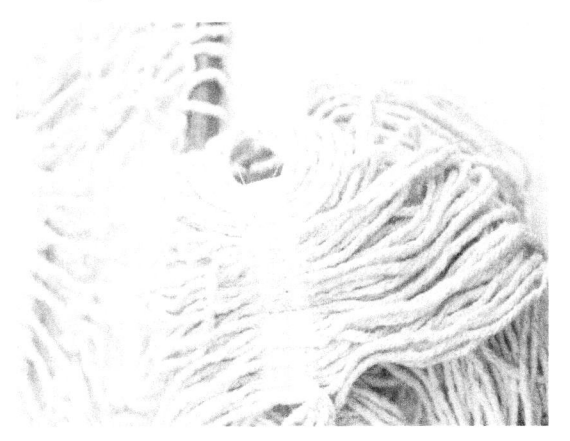

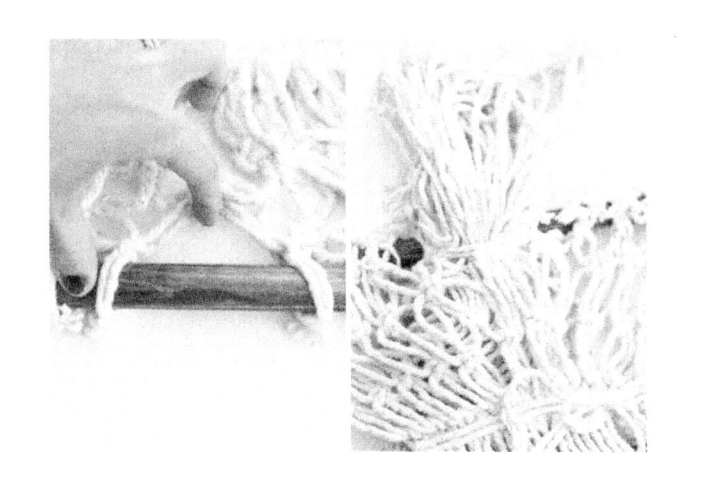

5: DIY Mini Macramé Wall Hanging (#5)

Tools and supplies

7 pieces of 4-foot long cord

Scissors

Wire brush

Instructions

1. Begin by cutting 7 equal pieces of cording, each measuring 4 feet long.

2. Then use Lark's Head knots to add the cording to the rings.

3. Make a series of diagonal half hitch knots from the two center cords. Ensure the first cord goes to the left side while the next knot to the right side.

4. Repeat the previous step to make another row of double half hitch knots. Continue from where you left off with another series of knots, but do diagonal half hitch knots this time. Your knots should go towards the center.

5. Repeat step 4 to make another row using the diagonal half hitch knots.

6. Complete your macramé design by fringing the hanging cords slightly using your wire brush.

7. Evenly cut your fringe cording to make the bottom neat. Begin making the square knot pattern.

8. Just cut 4 to 6 pieces of cording to approximately 4 feet long. Make a series of square knots in an alternating manner.

9. Make as many rows of knots as possible. Then use your wire brush to make a fringe —you could also make a row of half hitch knots.

6: Home Woven Wall Hanging in 5 Minutes

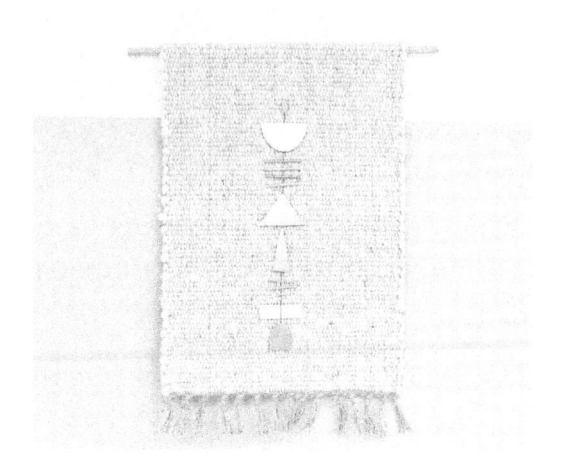

Tools and supplies

Dowel rod

Brass hanging piece

Yarn or twine

Stitch witchery OR and thread and a needle

2×3 woven rug

Iron, optional

Instructions

1. Cut a dowel rod down to the required size. Ensure the dowel is a few inches longer than your weaving width on all sides, a minimum of 12 inches.

2. Flip your rug over the side placed on the ground, and put a dowel rod on where it should end up. Add a strip of stitches below the dowel rod.

3. Place your iron in a furnace and fold over the top flap of your rug. Begin stitching the witchery as per the instructions; just run the hot iron over the top of the rug until the two pieces bond together. If the rug is extra thick, use a thread and needle instead.

4. Now tie a yarn piece to each side of your dowel rod and triple or double knot on each side of the rod.

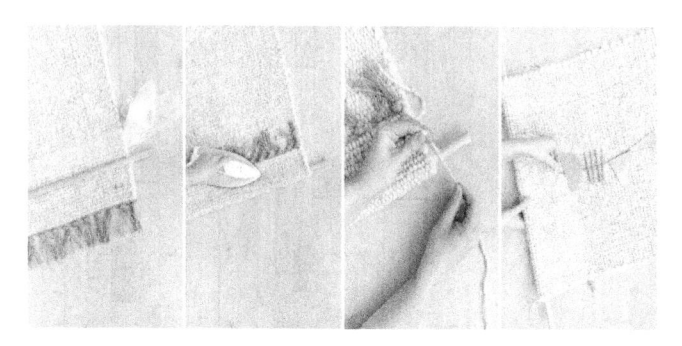

5. Cut off excess yarn or add a brass piece to each macramé design. You'll need to weave through a hole in the brass with another piece of yarn and a weaving opening in the rug. Try using double or triple knots.

7: Macramé Fiber Wall Art

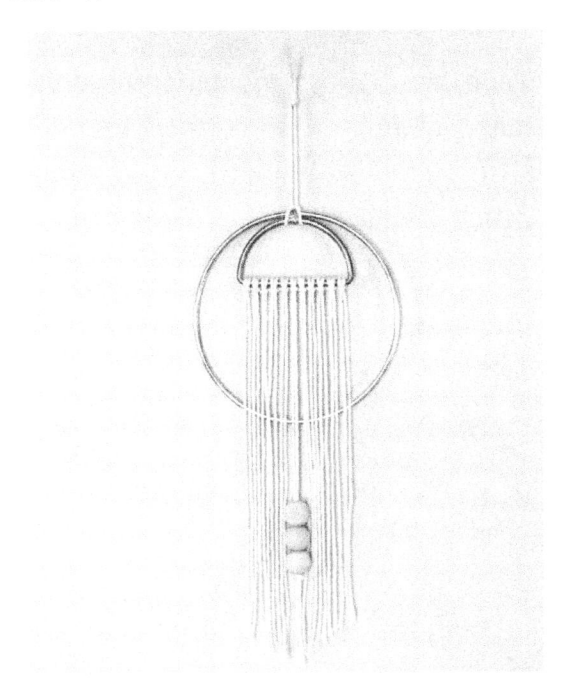

Tools and supplies

Wire

Wooden beads

String/yarn

D-ring

Metal hoop

Instructions

1. Attach the D-ring to the top of the hoop using the wire. Tightly wrap the wire around

the hoop and D-ring several times and secure by tucking behind.

2. Then cut about 11 equal lengths of yarn and make a loop around your D-ring. Try using a little glue on the back to keep the string from moving.

3. Start adding the beads. Just slide them over the two middle strings and tie a knot below them.

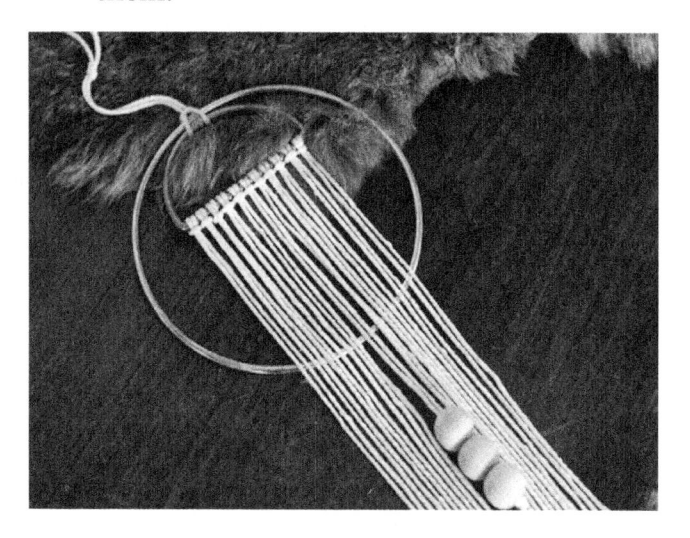

4. At this point, cut off the ends to create a design. You can make a loop of string around the top section and make a knot for hanging on the wall.

8: Macramé Wall Hanging in 20 Minutes

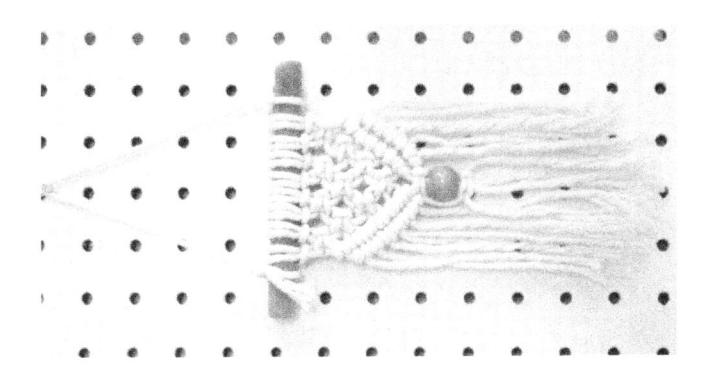

Tools and supplies

Eight 33-35 inches long strands of macramé cord

18 inches hanging strand of cord

5-8 inches wide driftwood, wood dowel, or stick

Wood bead, optional

Yarn needle, optional

Comb to brush fringe

Instructions

1. Start by cutting off 18 inches of the hanging cord and 8 strands of the macramé cord, each measuring 33-35 inches long.

2. Using the larks head knot, tie the 8 strands of cord around the wooden piece and then fold your cord in half. Grab the loop over the

top of the piece of wood and insert your fingers into the loop.

3. Pull the two strands of cord through and repeat this process for the entire bunch of 8 strands.

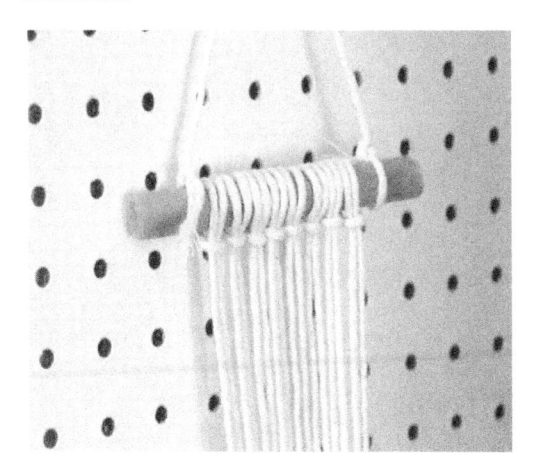

4. Make 4 square knots beginning with the 4 right or left strands. Leave the two left strands on the left in the next row and then create 3 square knots, followed by 2 knots and then one square knot.

5. Then grab the strand on the lead cord on the far right side and make a half hitch knot that goes diagonally to the middle.

6. Make one row comprising of half hitch knots from right to the center.

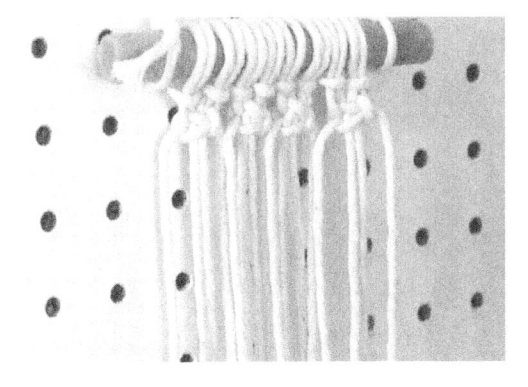

7. Make another row of half hitch knots starting from the left to the center. Repeat the step another time.

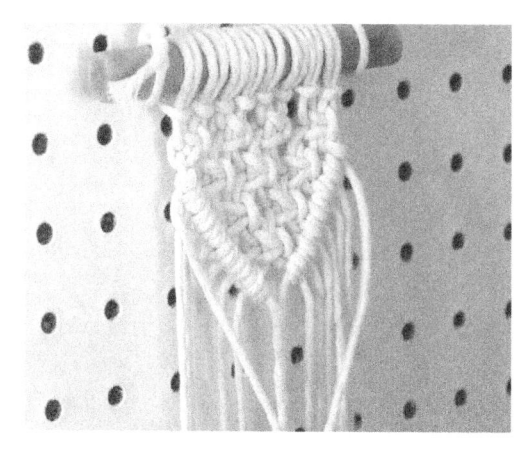

8. Pick the 4 pieces of lead cords and secure them using a square knot. Cut and comb fringe and now attach a wood bead if you like.

9: DIY Macramé Wall Hanging (#6)

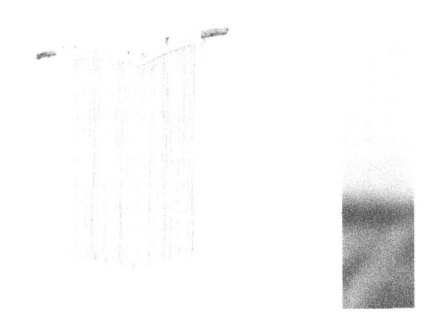

Tools and supplies

Scissors

Macramé cord

Wooden dowel

Glue

Instructions

1. Make the string you'll use to hang the macramé design. Just cut approximately 1 to 2 inches of cord and tie it around both

dowels' ends. Secure the rope using some glue.

2. Then tie a long thread of about 1 meter to the dowel. Cut a few 16cm long pieces of threads depending on your preferred color.

3. Tie the multicolored threads to the main long thread using a single knot. Repeat the step for about 40 rows or so.

4. Use a comb to tease the fibers of the feather to help them unravel. Then use the scissors to trim the threads into the shape of a feather.

5. At this point, loosen the main thread from your dowel, attach a bead on top of the feather's shape, and secure with glue.

6. Secure the main thread with the macramé feather design using the Larks Head Knot.

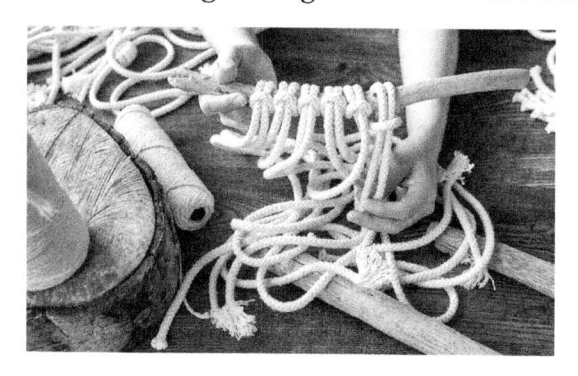

7. Create a few other macramé features and fix them on the dowel to create an aesthetic look.

10: Macramé Christmas Wreath

Tools and supplies

Fresh Greenery

Hot Glue Gun

Scissors

Macramé Cotton cords

Driftwood

Instructions

1. Get some scrap cords or yarn and driftwood pieces. Then shape out a tree from the driftwood and tie the corners with the cord, ensuring the cord touches all the corners.

2. Add enough macramé cords to create an attractive pattern. Use a few basic macramé knots to continue your pattern.

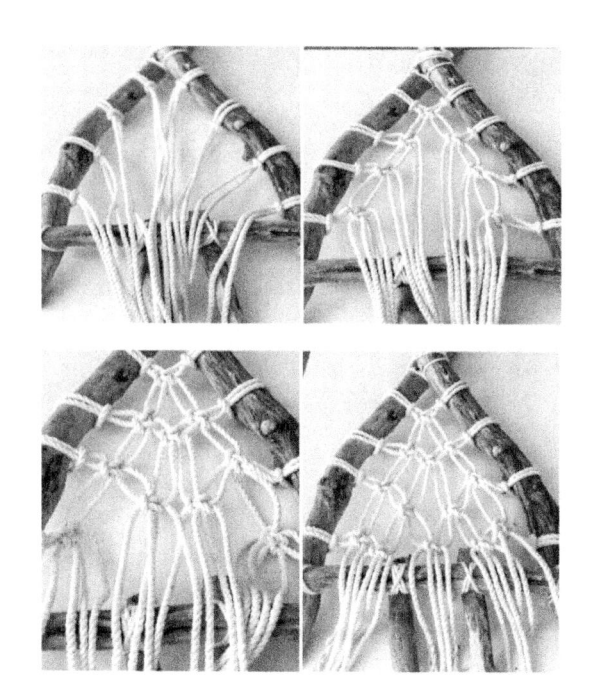

3. Then pull the unnecessary cords below the driftwood, and secure with some hot glue.

11: DIY Ring Wall Hanging

Tools and supplies

Yarn or Macramé String

2 gold rings, 8 inch and 6 inch

Scissors

Glue, optional

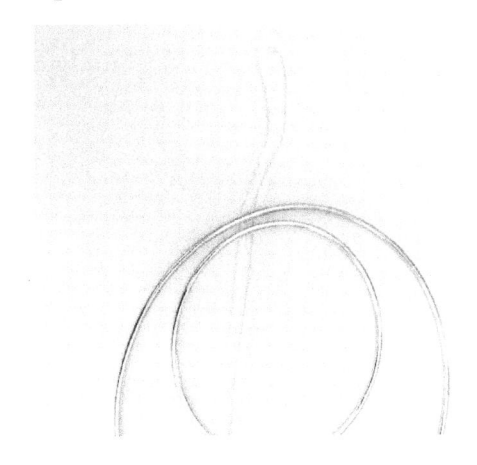

Instructions

1. Get a string or yarn, and then double it over to form a loop. Now run the yarn under the two rings to the back of the golden rings.

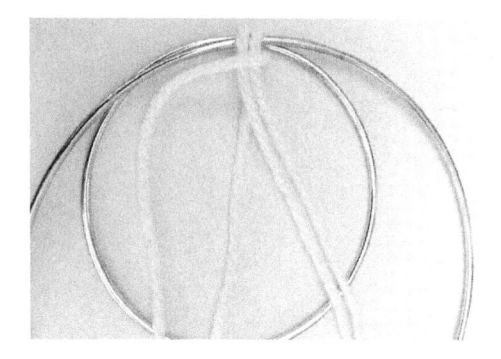

2. Then make a Lark's Knot with the yarn or string to tie the two golden rings. Wrap the yarn or string around both sides and secure the yarn with a knot.

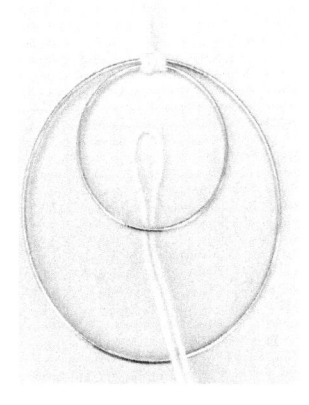

3. Double the yarn yet again and make another loop. Then make about 12 Lark's Knots or as needed.

4. As you make the knots, pull them tightly to ensure they sit securely on the gold ring.

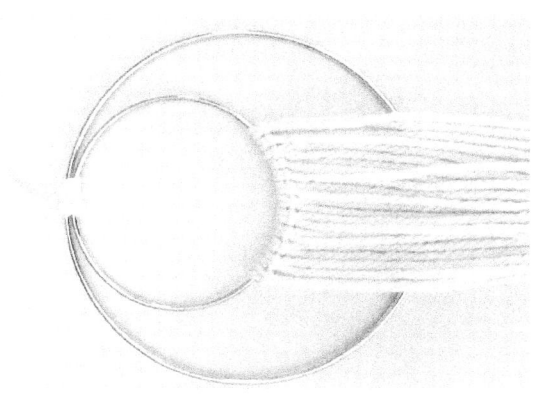

5. Cut off the yarn or string ends with your scissors.

12: DIY Yarn Wall Hanging

Tools and supplies

Different types and colors of yarn

12" brass hoop

5" brass hoop

Scissors

String

Instructions

1. Cut 8 strands of preferred yarn, each approximately 10 inches long.

2. Add the yarn pieces onto the bass hoop using the Lark's Knot, then trim the bottom.

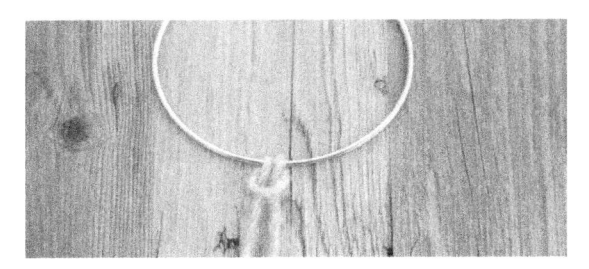

3. Cut approximately 25-30 yarn strands, each measuring 35 inches each, then attach each string piece to the hop through the Larks knot. Choose to either place colors randomly or as a pattern.

4. Pick the smallest hoop and carefully tie it inside the large hoop. Grab the string and wrap it 6-8 times on top of the two brass hoops to secure.

5. Finish with a double or triple knot.

13: Yarn Leftovers Wall Hanging

Tools and supplies

One or more colored yarn

Knitting needle or stick

Instructions

1. Begin by cutting your yarn to a uniform length depending on the knitting needle or stick length.

2. Fix the yarn onto the stick through lark's head knot and repeat this step until you have most parts of the stick covered. Leave a 1-inch allowance on both sides of the

string with which you'll hang the wall design.

3. At this point, tie other strings at each end of the stick, probably through a loop. Hang it!

14: Copper Wool Roving Macramé Wall Hanging

Tools and supplies

Nine 1-inch x 1/2 inch Copper Pipe Couplings

Sharp Sewing Scissors

Jute Twine or Cotton Crochet Thread

36 inches x 1 inch Wood Dowel, cut to 29 inches

1.1 lbs Merino Wool 40 mm, 33yds Per Ball

Floral Wire

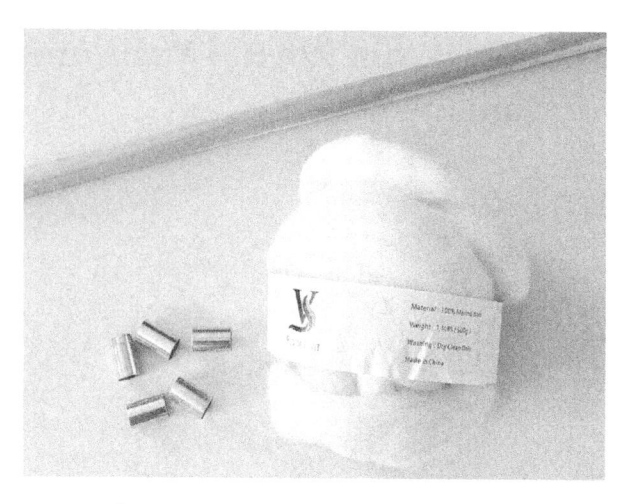

Instructions

1. Cut 7 strips of wool roving strips, each measuring 6 feet.

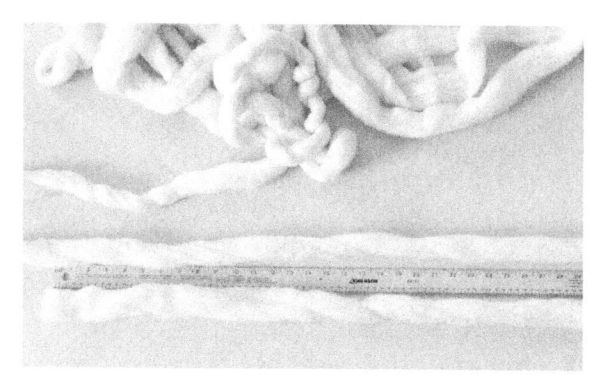

2. Then tie the wool roving strips around the wooden dowel through the Lark's Head Knots.

3. Evenly distribute the Lark's Head Knots and adjust them to uniform size. Cut some floral wire to 8 inches to help with attaching copper beads.

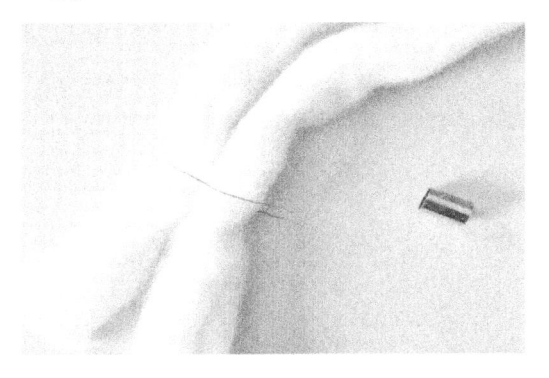

4. Now fold the floral wire in half and attach it to the end of both sections.

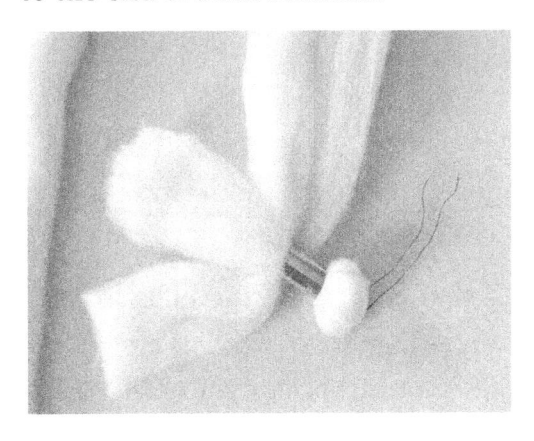

5. Pull the ends of your floral wire through the beads until the two ends go through the copper beads.

6. Then pull the copper bead up the wool roving and position it inches away from the top knot.

7. Add a copper bead to just one strand on the ends. The center strands should go into the beads about two at a go. Repeat the adding bead step across the eight strands.

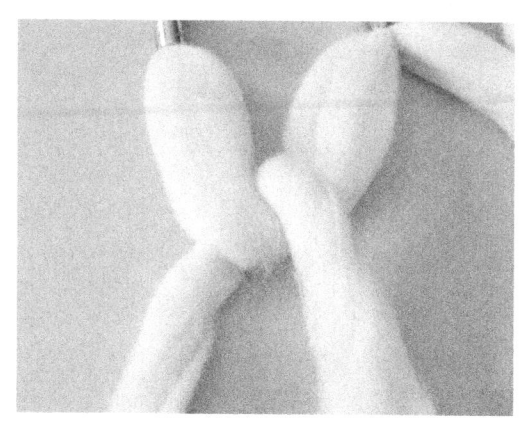

8. At about 5 inches below the beads, make a square knot into both strands positioned side by side.

9. At this point, fold the ends of the strands over twice and then pull them until snug. Do the knotting processes until you cover all

the strands. Ensure you evenly place or space all the knots and beads.

10. Next, pull the two strands from the second knot on the two sides and pull the strands through a copper bead.

11. Finally, fluff up individual strands and trim their ends nicely. Attach a cotton crotchet thread on both sides of your dowel for hanging.

15: Yarn Wall Hanging

Tools and supplies

4-foot wood dowel 1/2" diameter

1 ball of beige yarn

1 ball of colored yarn

Wood beads, optional

Scissors

Measuring Tape

Miter saw, or hand saw

Instructions

1. Cut your dowel to approximately 20 inches with a saw, then use your scissors to cut your beige yarn to about 28 inches.

2. Fix the yarn to individual ends of your wooden dowel using applicable knots.

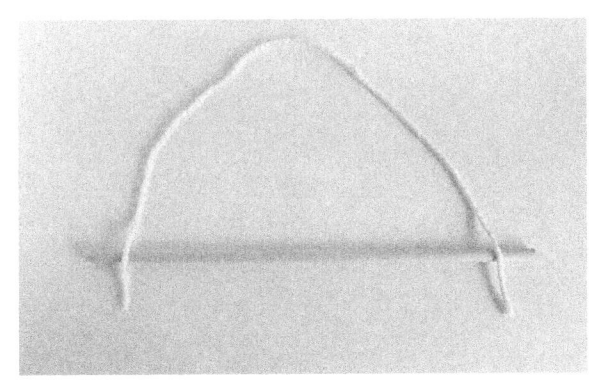

3. Now hook the dowel and the yarn onto a nail— you could also hook them to a wall.

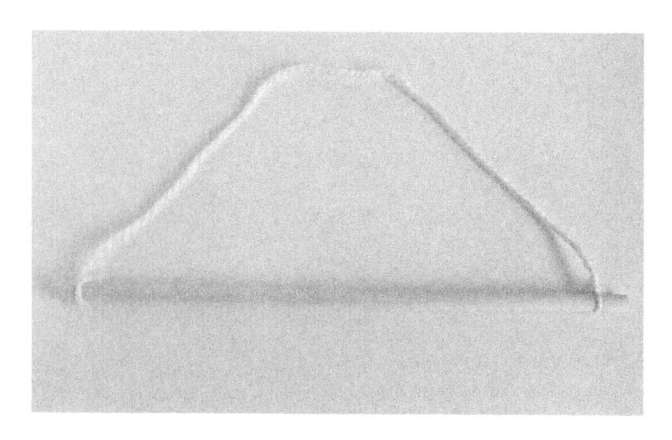

4. Cut 15 pieces of colored yarn, each 56 inches long.

5. Then pick three pieces of the yarn and loop them at the center onto the center of the wooden dowel. Tuck the 3 pieces of yarn into the loop to make a Lark's Head Knot.

6. Repeat step 5 until you obtain about 5 bunches from the 15 colored yarn pieces

attached to the wooden dowel through a Lark's Head Knot.

7. Now cut 18 pieces of the beige yarn with scissors, each measuring 48 inches.

8. Grab 3 beige yarn pieces right at the center and start looping them onto the dowel just adjacent to the colored yarn.

9. Repeat the previous step and put the beige yarn over the opposite side of the colored pieces of yarn.

10. Add more beige yarn on both sides of the colored yarn until you get 3 bunches of the beige-colored yarn on each side.

16: DIY Yarn Wall Hanging in 30 Minutes

Tools and supplies

10-inch pieces of driftwood

Self-striping yarn

A big book

A needle

Scissors

Instructions

1. Cut 140 strands of yarn, each measuring 28 inches, enough for four wall hangings.

2. Grab 4 yarn strands and fold them in half to create a loop. Put the created loop under the driftwood.

3. Pull the ends of the 4 yarn pieces through the loop as you go around the driftwood.

4. Grab another set of strands of yarn and tie them around the driftwood. Do this repeatedly 5 to 10 times until you're about to finish your wall hanging.

5. If you want to add some texture, add a few strands of yarn and make a simple macramé knot. Try making the knots as a 'V' shape.

17: DIY Macramé Plant Hanger

Tools and supplies

Hanging hoop

Ceiling hook

5 150" strands of string/yarn

Masking tape

Measuring tape

Scissors

Instructions

1. Begin by cutting 5 strands of strings measuring 150 inches long.

2. Now pick all your strands, align them, and insert a hoop onto the strings until it touches at the middle. Make a big knot.

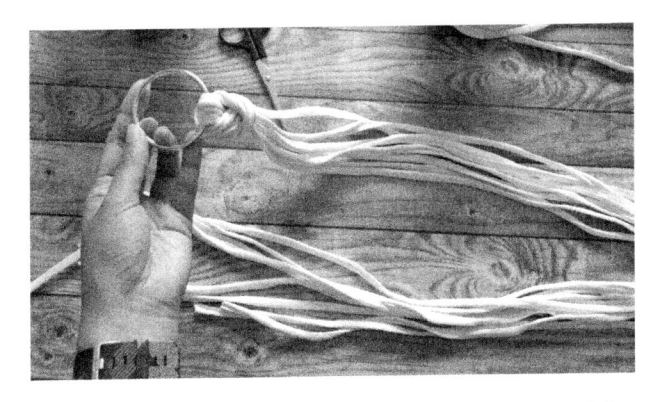

3. Grab a tape and tape your hoop to a tabletop to secure. Check if you have 1 string to work with. Organize the strings into 5 pairs.

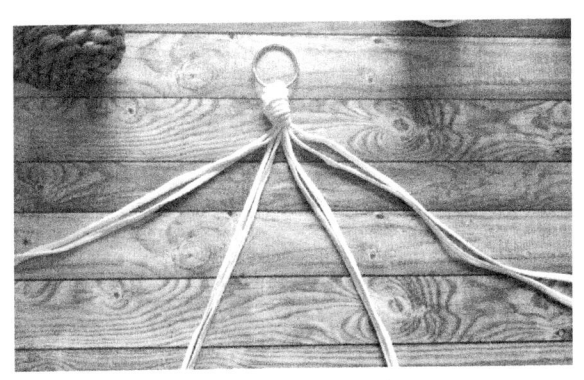

4. Begin knotting individual pairs right from 20 inches down from the topmost knot.

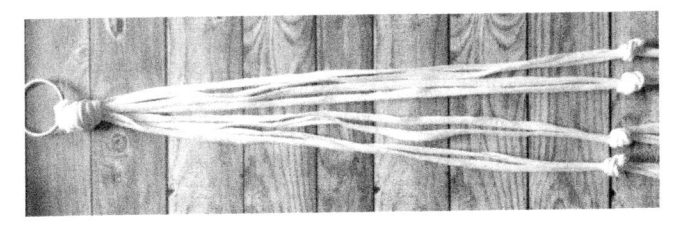

5. Pair individual string with the adjacent string and make more knots.

6. If you want your wall planter hanger to support a large or tall planter, you may make another set of knots, approximately 4 inches down from the last knots. Otherwise, skip this step.

7. Now make a large knot with all the strands approximately 2 inches down your last knot series.

8. You can now hang the wall plant hanger and carefully attach your planter.

18: DIY Macramé Wall Hanging (#7)

Tools and supplies

3-4′ wooden dowel

400 feet of thin rope

Tape

Fiskars Original Orange-handled Scissors

Instructions

1. Start by cutting your rope approximately 1 to 2 inches longer than your dowel, and then knot the rope at each end. You'll use this string to hang the design.

2. Cut 24 pieces of the rope, each 120 inches long, or based on your overall size of the macramé design.

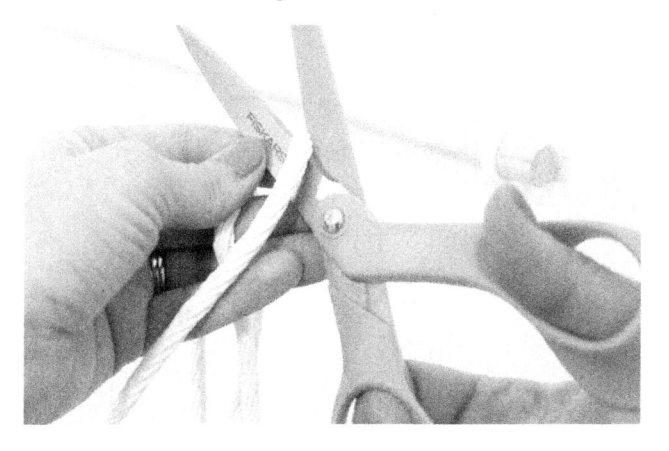

3. Now tie about 24 Lark's Head Knots across the entire wood dowel. Then, tie 12 square knots across the first row. Begin the knots on one end of your design and continue working across horizontally.

4. Skip the first two strands and the second row and begin making 11 square knots from the third strand. Continue knotting down

until you obtain a square knot at the center to create a "V" or triangle shape.

5. As soon as you have tied all rows with square knots, start making a set of diagonal double half hitch knots right from the right and left sides of your V or triangle shape.

6. By now, the knots should make a border, and you can trim out the V or triangle shape from your design. Check if you have any excess rope to make a fringe look at the bottom of the design.

7. At this point, tie another square knot at the bottom of the V shape to secure and join the double half hitch knots. To add more detail, grab four strands of the fringe in random areas and tie additional square knots.

8. Using your scissors and tape as your guide, diagonally trim the fringe to the preferred length.

19: DIY Modern Yarn Hanging

Tools and supplies

Yarn

7.25″ round wood dowel

1.5″ and 3″ gold rings

14″ cardboard

Krazy glue

Scissors

Instructions

1. Cut some yarn, fold it in half, then fix it through the 1½ inch gold ring.

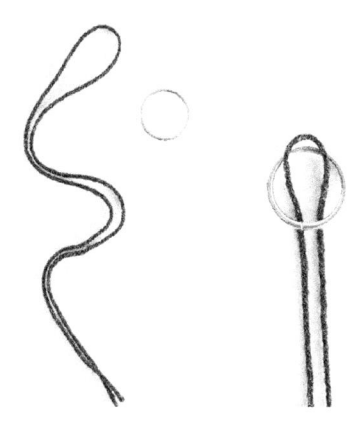

2. Grab the loose ends of the strings and pull them through the piece of yarn loop. Pull the string down and keep it loose: a lark's head knot.

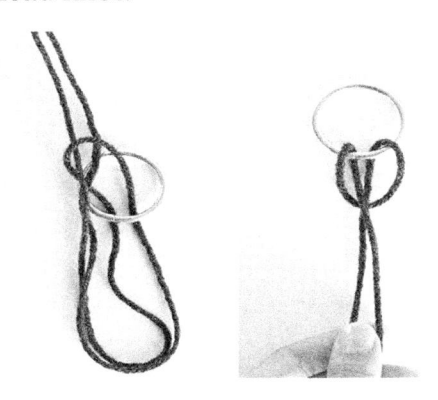

3. Now double knot the loose yarn ends to each wood dowel, and add a dab of glue to secure the knots. Cut down any excess yarn.

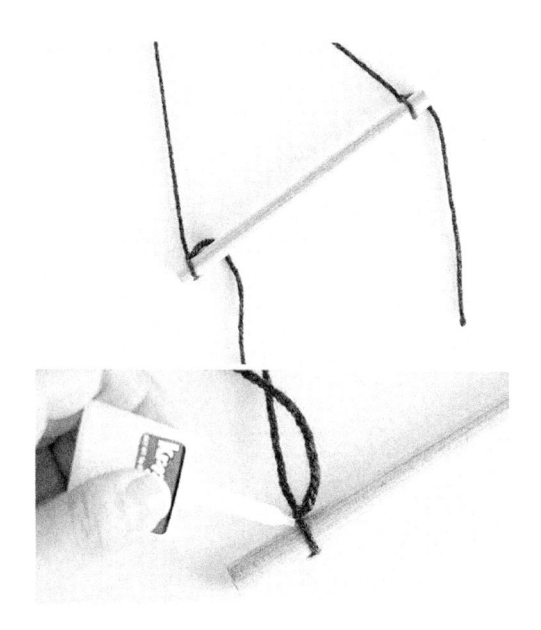

4. Grab a second folded yarn knotted on the other end, then tie a lark's head knot around the 3 inches ring. Pull the knot tight.

5. Pull the yarn through the first knot, then tie a lark's head knot around this knot.

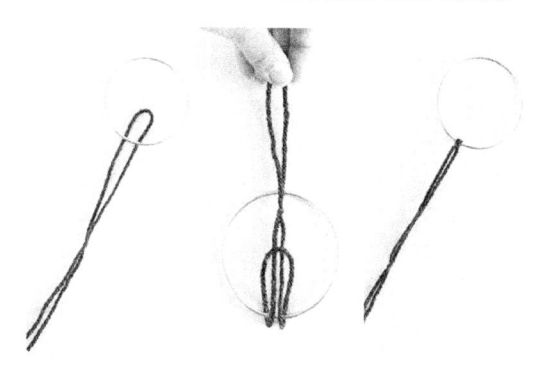

6. Pull it tight, reinforce with glue, and cut any unneeded yarn. Pull the first knot tight to reinforce the yarn on the ring.

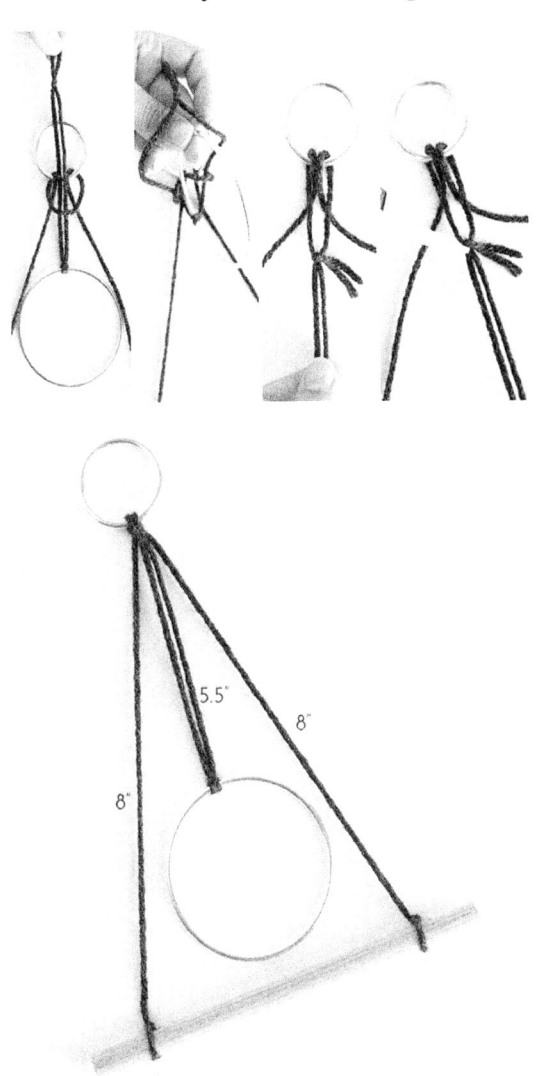

7. Cut a cardboard piece with a hacksaw approximately 14 inches long from a box. Use the cardboard to wrap your yarn about ten times.

8. If your yarn produces a half-folded cord or yarn bundle, cut down one end.

9. Make a big lark's head knot around your dowel to create 6 lark's head knots across the entire dowel, and pull each knot very tight.

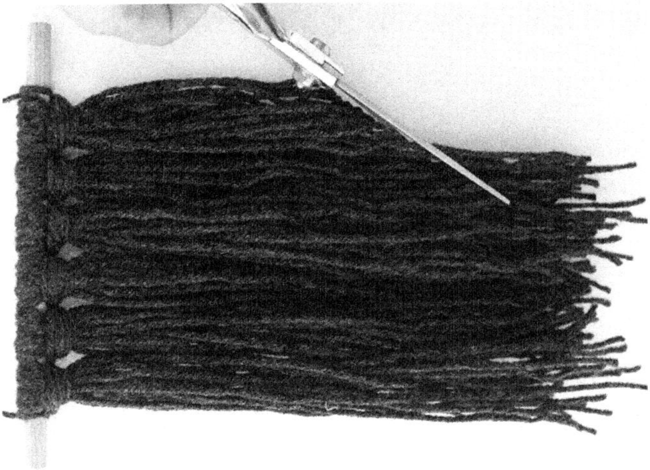

20: DIY Modern Macramé Wall Hanging

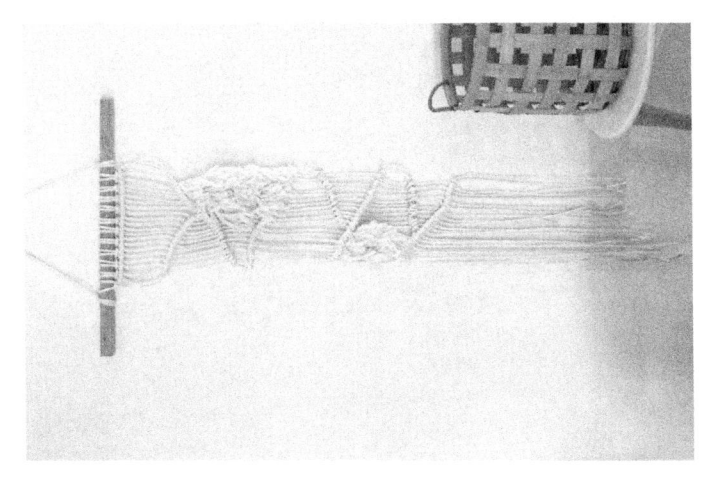

Tools and supplies

I ball Moda Vera Jester Yarn (cream)

35mm diameter Dowel cut to 60cm

50m x 6mm macramé cord

Scissors

Instructions

1. First cut 11 stands of macramé cord, each measuring 4.5 meters. Put the dowel somewhere accessible—perhaps between a stool and bookshelf.

2. Fold individual lengths of the macramé cord in half, and add it to the dowel through a

half hitch knot. Continue with the folding process until you attach all 11 cords.

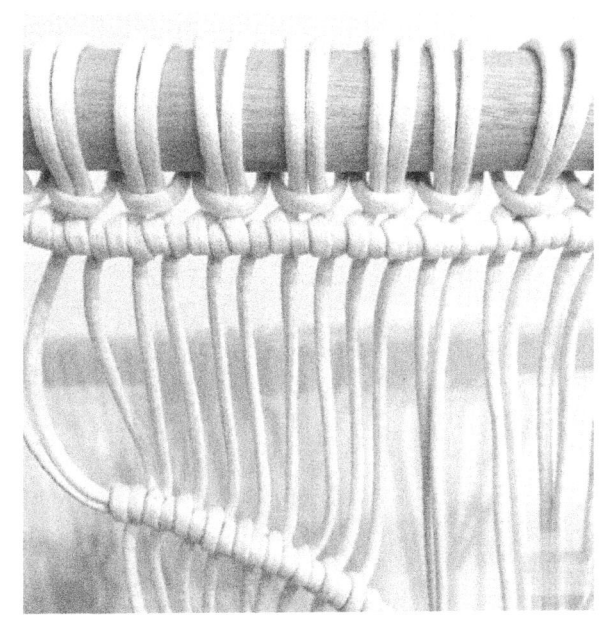

3. Now tie a horizontal half hitch knot across the top of the cords, and close your dowel.

4. Add extra texture to give it an organic look through a double half hitch. Create a series of Larks Head knots with the Jester wool.

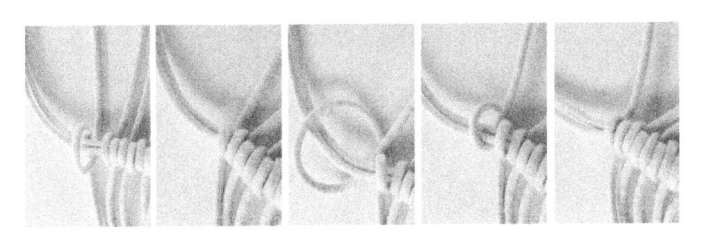

5. Then cut 3 pieces that measure 12cm each, and double over. Slide your loop around the macramé cords and pull the cord tails through the loop.

6. Continue the process until you obtain your pattern of choice. Cut the hanging cords at a diagonal.

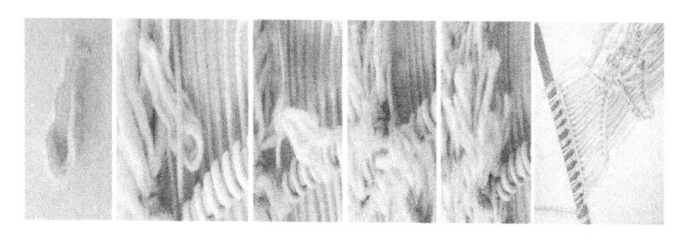

7. Finally, cut 3 lengths of the wool and make a double knot to secure each end. Tie the wool on both sides of your dowel before hanging.

Conclusion

As you have seen, making art pieces using macramé knots has never been easier! Go out, buy the required supplies, and begin practicing until you master this beautiful knot-tying crafting technique!

Printed in Great Britain
by Amazon